Poems Of Praise

Col 3:16 - Let the word of Christ dwell in you richly in all wisdom; teaching and admonishing one another in psalms and hymns and spiritual songs, singing with grace in your hearts to The LORD.

Poems Of Praise

By Steve Solomon

To order additional copies of this book, contact:
Xlibris
1-888-795-4274
www.Xlibris.com
Orders@Xlibris.com
799417

Contents

SPECIAL POEMS

<u>In loving memory of my mother, Lynn Solomon.</u>

<u>Sleep well, ye daughter of The Most High GOD.</u>

2 Corinthians 5:6-8: Therefore we are always confident, knowing that, whilst we are at home in the body, we are absent from The LORD: (For we walk by faith, not by sight:) We are confident, I say, and willing rather to be absent from the body, and to be present with The LORD.

Introduction

After publishing my first book in 2012, *A Rainbow Of Emotions* (ROE), I decided to continue writing. However, in the course of a few short years, there were a plethora of significant changes in my life that had drastic effects on my way of thinking. The most significant change of them all is that I had gone from being a believer (which *I* define as a person who believes that Jesus Christ is the Son of GOD) to a Christian (which *I* define as a person who has accepted Jesus Christ as their savior and is born again) and now a disciple of Christ (which *I* define as a person who not only worships The LORD Jesus, but also, as James 1:22 says, "But be ye doers of the word, and not hearers only, deceiving your own selves.",", applies and lives by the biblical principles).

Obviously, this has had a tremendous impact on my writing. This book reflects this transition as the poems have been written over the first four years of my salvation, and its contents are solely based on Christian ideology giving praise to our LORD and Savior Jesus Christ.

By publishing this book, I not only intend to give my brothers and sisters in Christ something both entertaining and inspirational to read, but I also hope that someone out there who is unsure of where they stand (spiritually) may find hope and strengthen their faith through the message of the gospel which has inspired me and had a tremendously positive impact on my life.

About This Book

This book is divided into three chapters. Chapter one is "Shorter Poems," which have less than six stanzas; each of which are based on a theme or concept. The poem "The Third Day," for example, is about the resurrection of Christ.

Chapter Two is "Longer Poems," which have six or more stanzas. These also have a central theme. The poem "Praise His Names," for example, uses many of the various names of Jesus.

Chapter Three is what I call "Special poems" and is broken up into six sections of various sizes. The name of each section indicates what is special about these particular poems. For example, the "Christmas" section are poems that were written for my Christmas cards.

There is one last thing I want to mention about this book: Three of the poems in this book are written in Spanish. While I do speak and understand some Spanish, I am not even close to being fluent, and I admit Google Translate played a significant part in the construction of those poems. With that said, for those who do not speak/read Spanish, I have followed each of them with the English translation.

And while the interior work of this book was constructed and compiled by me, I must recognize and give a "grandiose expression of exemplary gratitude" to the three brethren who have also contributed their time and effort to the final product of this book. First, I thank my two proofreaders whom The LORD hath verily blessed with the gift of His wisdom (who have requested to remain anonymously out of the spotlight) and have been an abundant blessing to me and my walk with Christ! I would also like to thank my brother-in-Christ, Dan Pellegrino Jr., from kingdomimpactdesign.com for designing the cover art for this book. Truly, The LORD hath blessed him with the patience to work with me to come up with the finished product you hold in your hand. Without them being the furnace to this work, this would be a lump of unrefined gold with the dross still inside. May The LORD shower you three with blessings and an abundance of grace!

Chapter One

SHORTER POEMS

Called to Fight

People meet me today, and they see what I have become,
But those new people have no idea where I'm coming from.
They say "pleased to meet you" to the man I am today,
But I doubt they would say that to the man I was yesterday.

Although the things I've done and learned will always remain,
The way that I approach them has forever been changed.
Who I will be is not who I am, and who I am is not me from the past;
Each one having part of the others, but each one wiser than the last.

Now that I'm older, I am now able to look back in retrospect;
All the situations and my decisions, I can think back to and reflect.
I've seen and felt the damage and pain that living in sin can bring:
Anger, greed, and envy can destroy the things of which you dream.

But what I can see now is that I was meant to walk that road in life,
Grow up a happy kid and, in adolescence, discover the world's strife;
Diving in and embracing an angry world full of evil, violence, and hate.
It wasn't The LORD's but the way of the world that I started to imitate.

But even despite the fact that I was going down a dark and dismal path,
My Savior came and drove the enemy away and saved me from his grasp.
Now my GOD has called me to use what I've learned; for Him, I am to fight.
I know what lurks in the darkness, but it's there I bring the light.
The enemy may try one of his many tricks or try a sneak attack,
But I'm not worried, for who can stand against me if Jesus has my back?
Amen.

Imagine a Treasure

Imagine a treasure so vast it's deeper than all the seven seas.
Imagine a treasure so abundant you can share it with everyone you meet.
Imagine a treasure so fulfilling it allows everyone to feel complete.
Imagine a treasure that is infinite and can never run out or deplete.

Imagine a treasure that doesn't decay; it lasts forever and ever.
Imagine a treasure so amazing it doesn't get any better.
Imagine a treasure so glorious it's worth any and every endeavor.
Imagine a treasure that is yours, from which you'll never sever.

Imagine a treasure at the end of a straight and narrow road.
Imagine a treasure, a marvelous mansion, a holy abode.
Imagine a treasure eternal no moth can eat nor rust corrode.
Imagine a treasure no thief can steal nor will time erode.

Imagine a treasure full of both ancient and brand new things.
Imagine a treasure O, the infinite joy and jubilation that it brings.
Imagine a treasure so amazing that all of the heavenly host sings.
Imagine a treasure, spending forever with Jesus, The King of Kings.

My Savior

The King of Kings is my personal Savior.
For The LORD I keep to my best behavior.
To humbly serve The LORD fills my heart with joy.
It's His commandments and laws I employ.
In His name do I joyfully work and labor.

Praising His name and seeking His favor;
Helping the needy and loving my neighbor.
My afflictions, The Almighty delivers me from and destroys.
His discernment makes the wisest men seem as mere boys.
I study His word written on sacred paper.

Wielding the scripture as a spiritual rapier,
His sword cutting through evil like a holy razor.
When the devil attacks and tries to provoke and annoy,
I raise myself up to battle against the adversary I deploy,
Stopping the devil in his tracks like a powerful taser.

His vengeance turning His servants' enemies to vapor,
His love and mercy are the sweetest of sweet savors.
Faith despite hardship empowers me to keep my poise;
The adversary may try to tempt me, but all I hear is noise.
No temptation or hardship can cause my faith to waver.

Soldiers of Christ

Soldiers Of Salvation, soldiers of Christ,
Anointed to serve our GOD in His name;
His name is not once, but He who is thrice;
He is The lion of Judah no one can tame.

When the devil comes to steal and destroy
And the accuser of brethren comes toward,
The name of our mighty Savior we deploy,
For He came to bring not peace but a sword.

When the enemy of man comes to attack,
We fear not and charge to the front line;
We drive that serpent of old right back,
Crushing the head of the father of lies.

Anointed to become satan's nightmare
With fervent intercession and prayer,
In Jesus's name engage in spiritual warfare,
The blood of The Lamb gets him scared.

The Third Day

This time of Easter, when in remembrance of Him,
We give thanks, break the bread, and raise the cup
Because on Calvary's cross, the victory He did win.
They destroyed the temple, and in three days, He rose it up.

We celebrate when The LORD gave the price for all sin,
Out of love gave Himself to be the final Passover Lamb
For both the Jews and gentiles, of all nations and kin.
Who can redeem our salvation but the Son of Man?

He went to the cross and endured its suffering for us.
He sacrificed so that, at His side, we can eternally remain.
He is true to His word, and His promise, we will trust.
He will wipe away every tear and relieve every pain.

No greater love Hath He to lay down His life for His friends.
He laid down His life that He might take it again.
The good Shepherd loved His sheep until the very end.
The faith of Christ with our lives we will always defend.

We will go out to preach the gospel and tell His story.
We honor The LORD Jesus and bless His holy name.
We worship Him and give Him all the praise and glory.
Our Savior's love, we will forever publicly proclaim.

We Are Soldiers

We are Soldiers Of Salvation, The LORD's chosen people.
We are servants of The Almighty GOD of Israel who has no equal.
Going out to spread the word and feeding the hungry,
He is the One true living GOD, the eternal Holy Trinity.

We preach the gospel that all may give glory to The LORD.
We are prayer warriors wielding His spiritual sword,
Soldiers marching in the army of the Holy Trinity.
When there is any type of need, call on SOS ministry.

Christ came for us to have life more abundantly;
Day after day, sometimes it may seem like redundantly.
A ministry of giving, we seek opportunities to serve,
Sharing the news of His grace that no human deserves.

We are Soldiers Of Salvation, defenders of the faith.
We are Soldiers Of Salvation, guardians of the saints.
Being our brother's keeper but doing it with love,
Keeping to the commandments of our Father above.

You Are Jehovah

You are The LORD, my peace, Jehovah-Shalom.
You are GOD, He who sits on the throne.
Throughout the earth, let Your glory be shown.
In You, I live, move, and have my being alone.

You are The LORD, my banner, Jehovah-Nissi.
Your voice is as the roaring of the seven seas.
There is none greater or mightier than Thee.
You are the strength that abides inside of me.

You are Jehovah-Rapha, The LORD, my healer.
You are the original hidden truth revealer,
The Good Shepherd, the lost soul retriever.
Of Your sword of The Spirit, I am now a wielder.

You are Jehovah-Jireh, The LORD, my provider.
There is no name under heaven that is higher.
You abundantly grant my needs and desires.
O LORD GOD, fill me with Your Holy Ghost fire.

You are Jehovah-Tsabaoth, The LORD of Hosts.
Baptize me in the power of The Holy Ghost.
Separate me from sin, far as coast is from coast.
In my heart, serving You is absolutely foremost.

Un Fuego en mi Corazon

Tengo un fuego en mi corazón que arde brillante.
Un pasión por buscar y servir vigilente.
Hacer la voluntad de Dios es mi propósito en la tierra.
Y a para proclamar Su gloria desde toda sierra.

Puedo escuchar el sonido de la bocina en mi alma.
La voz del SEÑOR me llama a la batalla.
El fuego del Espíritu arde en mis venas.
Estando lleno de Su poder que rompe todas las cadenas.

Soy un soldado que marchando en el nombre de Jehovah de Los Ejércitos.
Mis armas son la fe, la oración y los santos manuscritos.
Mi Vida está en Sus manos, soy Tuyo para mandar.
Dondequiera que me dirija, ahí traigo la luchar.

Tengo un fuego en mi Corazón por la guerra.
El enemigo, en un círculo de fuego yo encierra.
Quemando con un pasión por la batalla.
Cuando voy al altar el enemigo estalla.

Todo la dia con la espada del espíritu en mis manos.
Peleando el adversario en oración con mis hermanos
Yo reprendo el diablo con fuego y azufre.
Y reclamó el sangre de Cristo para que mis hermanos están asegure.

Chapter Two

LONGER POEMS

Battle Cry

Jesus came not to bring peace but a sword,
So this is a declaration of war in the name of The LORD.
All powerful GOD who parted the seas,
O Prince of Peace, my enemies are under Your feet.

Awesome GOD of power, might, and glory,
LORD mighty in battle, come and fight for me.
Against *all* evil powers and principalities,
Against the wicked one, I declare war in the heavenlies.

Hear my cry, Jehovah, protector of my family.
I claim the blood of Jesus against the enemy.
Almighty GOD, fill my vessel with Your light;
Empower your servant against the enemy's strife.

In my heart, the joy of The LORD shall abound.
I'm done playing games, no more fooling around.
The gloves are off, and the ropes are on the ground.
This sparring match is over, devil, you're going down.

No longer will my Savior allow me to be deceived,
For the word of GOD, in my heart, I have received.
Shakinah glory, sword of the Spirit unsheathed,
Now upon you, satan, may GOD's wrath be unleashed.

Boldly declaring war against the enemy,
Conquering the devil to reclaim prosperity,
Spiritual violence and sanctified hostility,
In His mighty name to Kingdom victory.

You know the devil really gets nervous
Because he knows he is unable to hurt us
When we rebuke him; we know he heard us
When we are fervent in Holy Spirit service.

Marching to the altar, ready for war,
Kneeling in prayer, drawing His sword;
Together with brethren in one accord,
claiming victory in the name of The LORD.

Culture Clash

A differentiation apparently not so common place,
The distinction between culture, religion, and race.
For many, there are that think they are one andthe same.
Anyone who disagrees with them is met with disdain.

Religion is the practice of a person's spiritual belief,
A higher power that comforts them in times of grief;
Worshiping, praying, giving praise and sacred rituals;
Ceremonial garments, observing holy days and dedicated victuals.

Culture is music, dancing, games, family structure, and food;
Deciding what things are considered bad and which ones are good.
Architecture, climate, fashion, vegetation and kinds of crops;
It's whether problems are handled peacefully or by firing of shots.

One's race is the genealogy of their forefathers' bloodline,
Their heritage and ancestry from the beginning of time;
Those living now being fruit of their family tree,
Until the day the fruit falls to multiply its seed.

Through the passage of time, these concepts have been blurred;
For when one is inquired of, it is usually all three that are heard;
For religion contributes to culture, and both are learned by a parent's voice.
But what is never taught is that unlike heredity, religion and culture
are a choice.

Most people follow in their parents' footsteps and do what worked for them,
But sometimes a disdain for the lessons learned in youth begins to stem.
One's race is written in stone, but religion and culture are subject to change.
If a child disagrees with a parent's beliefs, their practices get rearranged.

To say that race, religion, and culture are all one and the same
Shows that person lacks the ability to engage their brain.
To deny these distinctions is the mark of an arrogant fool;
Some use the ignorance of the youth as a recruiting tool.

Most people don't realize that they are being enslaved,
Warnings against outside influences elders rant and rave;
Society enforcing belief in fiction like Santa and his elves,
They are intimidated by those who think for themselves.

Culture clash happens when someone questions what they are told,
Finding a path that contradicts the cultural package they've been sold.
While many children blindly follow the path their parents have paved,
There are those who search for a path of their own despite the waves.

Culture is like science in that it constantly adapts and evolves,
Straying from one's parents' path leads to inner conflict resolved.
What works for one person doesn't work for them all;
Trying to explain this to some people is like talking to a wall.

Doors and Windows

There are times in life we feel down and have our doubts,
Unpleasant situations that cause us to look for a way out,
Things and people that make us want to scream and fight,
Circumstances that make us feel like we are locked up tight.

In these times, we must not walk by sight but rather by faith.
When we trust in The LORD, He shows us there is always a way.
"GOD doesn't close a door without opening a window," so it is said,
For Him, nothing is impossible, even restoring life to the dead.

When life puts you into a room and all the exits seem locked,
Turn your trust in The LORD, and your path will become unblocked.
He may loose the obstruction and unlock a window or door,
But He can also create an open space where a wall once stood before.

It may seem that barred are the windows and locked are the doors,
But remember the chains that bound Peter, and always trust in The LORD.
In a prison, he was kept; and between two guards, he was chained;
But all the doors and gates opened for him because he never lost faith.

Like at the walls of Jericho, GOD instructed that the trumpets sound,
And the enemy's invincible defenses came crumbling to the ground.
What would normally seem impossible is nothing for Him to do,
So when you are suffering affliction, just have faith He will deliver you.

Jehovah is Almighty; there's nothing beyond His awesome power.
With faith the size of a mustard seed, even a mountain will run and cower.
Jesus is a mighty warrior; He is our fortress and our strong tower.
He is our Savior, and He is the light that shines on us in our darkest hour.

The LORD created all things, and without Him was not anything made.
He is our shelter when things of the world try to rain on your parade.
He gave us dominion over the earth, but over us, He does reign.
This is why we worship and glorify Him, praising His holy name.

We are all His children, though we are only flesh and blood,
But when we give Him our faith, with blessings He does flood.
Sometimes He tests us, and He will put obstacles in our way,
But He gives us strength to overcome that we may demonstrate our faith.

We must remember that Christ is our King and is always by our side.
He will never abandon us that we should suffer and be miserable in life.
We may not see His ways, for they are not meant for us to understand.
That doesn't mean He isn't still protecting us with His mighty hand.

He places unseen opportunities that lay in wait just around the bend,
And when we are in above our heads, His angels he will send.
If you accept that Jesus shed His blood for you when He died upon the cross,
You will achieve salvation and overcome every obstacle you come across.

Just like the nations that stood between the Hebrews and the Promised Land,
There is nothing of this earth or even the devil that can withstand.
Even if it seems that all the windows and doors appear to be locked,
Remember to have faith in The LORD whose power cannot be stopped.

Inches and Miles

The abundance and generosity of The LORD is amazing.
Jesus blesses and provides us with so many great things.
Even when overwhelming anxiety and anger has us pacing,
He supports and guides us through everything we're facing.

There are some cultures that are raised up consumed with greed.
It's those people GOD makes by cobwebs their money supersede.
His humble servants asks for only what they actually need.
Because of their faith, double portions is what they receive.

When you use what you have to try to make others smile,
When you ask GOD for an inch, instead He will give you a mile;
To the generous person, The LORD's blessing will be piled,
But for those that value fortune and fame lies fate most vile.

No matter how difficult life may get or how horrible things seem,
The shoulder of Christ is always there for us to cry and lean.
Regardless of what tragedy strikes, I know I'm on the winning team.
That's how I can be sure that if my foot slips, I can be redeemed.

Through faith, all things are possible by the power of Jesus Christ.
In times that are tough, He lifts us up to unimagined heights.
When the wicked one attacks, He is the one who wins all the fights.
Blessings beyond imagination He gives for doing what is good in His
sight.

There is no limit to the blessings that The LORD can bestow and yield.
We are the laborers in His vineyards and the fruit of His fields.
Faith, prayer, and His word are the weapons that I choose to wield
Because against the wickedness of the world, Christ is my shield.

The Father blesses us in abundance with things we never expected,
Even when everyone around makes me feel like socially rejected.
By fellow servants of The LORD, I am always welcomed and accepted.
To Jesus Christ, my LORD and Savior, I will never be disconnected.

When it comes to serving the LORD of Lords, I am full of zeal.
There is no comparison to the bliss that He causes me to feel.
When things get out of control, I just let GOD take the wheel.
All those that seek to cause me harm, he grinds them under heel.

When the road seems impossible, He shows us how to go.
His love is more beautiful than the brightest of rainbows.
There is nothing that He cannot see or does not know.
For His servants that reap faith, victory is what He sows.

Although of The Truth, The Life, and The Way many are naïve,
They were never taught properly, or they have been deceived;
But nothing that can convince me in Christ I should not believe.
For my unwavering faith, miles of blessings I have already received.

Mysterious Ways

The LORD certainly works in the most mysterious ways.
By His wisdom, He puts everything into its proper place.
His grand design is beyond our wisdom and comprehension.
He knows when to put pressure and when to relieve tension.

He knows what we need more than we know it ourselves,
All the people and things that are good for our spiritual health.
Sometimes He blesses us with our heart's deepest desires,
And at others, He chastens us with His consuming fire.

Sometimes we ask and pray for things that we never receive,
But in His judgments, we must always trust and believe.
If our Heavenly Father denies us our most passionate request,
He does so because, for us, those things are not what is best.

When The LORD blesses us, He does so in great abundance,
Showering us with blessings and removing our encumbrance.
Jesus is our protector, our provider, and our rewarder;
Rejuvenating us with the power of His living water.

He guides us to all the places that we need to be
And sends to us the people that we need to meet.
Our LORD deeply loves us, and He wants to show it,
Even when He gives us chances and we blow it.

Blessing us with His loving kindness and mercy,
Sustaining us when we are hungry and thirsty;
Blessed are those who are His humble servants,
Giving ourselves to Christ with a love ever fervent.

When in His eternal wisdom we have no doubt,
It is simply amazing how everything works out;
Answering our prayers when the time is right,
Empowering us when the enemy tries to fight.

Though we may not understand His glorious ways,
We magnify the name of Jesus for all of our days.
Too many are blind to His magnificent perks,
Taking for granted all the miracles that He works.

There is no god above Him, no other worthy of our praise.
He sacrificed His only begotten Son that we might be saved;
Blessing us by manifesting the dreams deep in our hearts,
His shield of faith quenching the enemy's fiery darts.

If our prayers go unanswered, there is a good reason,
For The LORD always provides for us in our due season.
Those who serve our LORD shall never be in lack.
On His children, our Heavenly Father will never turn His back.

Never Alone

My family is my heart.
The LORD is my soul.
If I was alone, I'd fall apart,
But clearly, this is not so.

I may sit or walk by myself,
But that doesn't mean I'm alone.
Aiding those that need help,
Christ watches over me from His throne.

With my purpose, in life I'm in touch.
I know I was born for a reason,
Giving to those that don't have as much.
Serving The LORD is never out of season.

I may be ostracized for my belief,
Criticized for all my choices,
But my Savior always provides relief,
So I praise Him with my loudest of voices.

If serving GOD was easy, then everyone would serve,
But entrance to the kingdom of heaven can't be earned.
Salvation is a privilege nobody ever deserves.
Those that fail are cast out to be eternally burned.

He spilled His blood and gave His life for us.
His only begotten Son sacrificed upon the cross.
In The Father, The Son, and Holy Ghost, I trust.
He gave my life purpose when I was lost.

Our Heavenly Father watches over us all.
Giver of guidance and unconditional love,
He is there to catch us if we slip and fall,
Always protecting us from the heavens above.

Until I welcomed Jesus into my heart,
I really didn't know what I was missing.
In the grand design, He gave me my part.
For peace and joy, I need no longer be wishing.

Every day I give praise to His holy name,
Kneeling before Him to worship The LORD.
Over this world, He is the one that reigns;
Deliverance and glory known across the board.

Praise His Names

His names are all worthy of praise.
He is The Truth, The Life, and The Way;
Jesus of Nazareth, King of the Jews.
I am denouncing all others; it's His path, I choose.

The Father, The Son, and The Holy Ghost,
He is the one that has sacrificed the most.
For our sins, He gave his only begotten Son
That we might be saved when His Kingdom come.

Jehovah is The LORD; He is The Son of Man.
For His glory, I joyfully do everything I can.
The LORD of Lords and King of Kings
Sanctified glory that only Immanuel brings.

Jesus Christ is my personal Savior.
He is The Almighty, The holy Creator,
Lion of Judah, The Preserver, The Intercessor,
The Good Shepherd, The all-merciful, and Protector.

The Son of Mary, The Son of GOD;
The Good Shepherd who comforts me with His rod;
The Alpha and Omega, The Word made flesh;
For The Prince of Peace, I always give my best.

The Redeemer, The Dove, The Door,
Nothing and no one can stand before
The King of Glory, Author of all things.
It is salvation that The Messiah brings.

The Light of the World, The Bread of Life;
He is The Sacrificial Lamb that paid the ultimate price.
The Eternal, The Risen, The Anointed;
I ask, and I receive. I'm never disappointed.

The Lamb of GOD, The Only begotten;
What You sacrificed will never be forgotten.
The Comforter, The Consoler The True Vine,
The Incarnation of the Most Divine.

The Absolute, The Man of Sorrows;
Our time on this earth is only borrowed.
He is The Word, The Infinite, THAT I AM.
We must praise His names while we can.

Stumbling Blocks to Stepping Stones

The life of every Christian has its ups and its downs.
We have moments when we smile and moments we frown.
The servants of The LORD, the devil tries corrupting,
But when we walk in faith, Christ Jesus is interrupting.

The enemy sets stumbling blocks before us,
But I guess he doesn't know
The LORD goes continually before us,
Turning them into stepping stones.

The enemy may place obstacles to block our path
Or try deceiving us into making a golden calf.
Believers walk according to their heart and not their eyes.
For riches of this world, our salvation we won't jeopardize.

Against our salvation, the powers of hell will fight,
But The LORD shall bring their darkness into the light.
They use the things and people around us to turn our hearts astray,
But our faith keeps us focused on The Truth, The Life, and the Way.

There are times in life you need to make a choice.
You can follow the crowd or stand up and raise your voice,
But when the world seems against us unless we conform,
That's when we act in faith and, in Jesus's name, perform.

No matter what, our Savior always has our back.
Our King raises up to block the enemy's attack.
Through Jesus Christ, all things are possible.
He has conquered satan and sent him to the hospital.

Demons may come intending to steal our peace,
But the glory of The LORD shall never cease.
We keep His praises close to us in our heart.
He's had the greatest love for us since the very start.

Though our salvation, the forces of evil will try to stop.
But, Jehovah, You place my feet upon the rock.
No matter what circumstances may get in the way,
Above all our afflictions, it is us The LORD shall raise.

Even we succumb to illness or wind up in bandages,
GOD will turn all our problems into advantages.
The LORD is my strong tower by which I am saved when I run,
For there is nothing in all creation He can't overcome.

No matter however hard, the devil tries and tries,
There is no obstacle the enemy is able to devise.
Whether well planned out or improvised,
That can overcome the power of Jesus Christ.

The Commander

I am a soldier, fighting in the eternal army.
Try as he might, the enemy can never harm me.
I live my life in service to The Commander.
His will be done in the face of mockery and slander.

Christ is our Commander that we serve with love,
Receiving His orders from the heavens above.
For The LORD, our Commander and Chief,
We strengthen our resolve and unswerving belief.

We march in His army, fighting the good fight;
Worshiping, praying, and praising Him day and night.
Faith, prayer, and scripture are my weapons of battle.
Without them, I'd be up the creek without a paddle.

We fight for The Commander in all His glory.
We're spreading His word and telling His story,
Sharing our increase to keep the hungry from starvation,
Praising His name, doing His will, and achieving salvation.

When the rapture arrives, He will come to collect His church.
To be collected at that time, it's the scripture we must research.
Our Commander is The Almighty, the first and the last.
If you serve the adversary, into the fire you'll be cast.

We fight for our Commander and always take His side.
Even in the face of persecution, our faith will never be denied,
Accepting missions and following His orders without question,
Claiming all that which He has given to us for our possession.

Protecting us and providing everything that we need,
Keeping His promises like multiplying Abraham's seed;
He grants us everything that our hearts desire,
A guardian ever watchful that never sleeps or grows tired.

The Commander knows what we need and always provides.
When the enemies attack, by His hand, they meet their demise.
We fight for Him as He protects us from our enemies.
The Commander banishes devils, demons, and principalities.

Giving what we can and helping the needy,
Living with generosity and not being greedy;
One who serves The Commander is never bored.
We live by the phrase "prepare ye the way of The LORD."

The LORD giveth and The LORD taketh away;
We praise His name until the rapture, the end of days.
No matter how many people blaspheme and slander,
From now until forever, He will always be my Commander.

The Grand Design

The Holy Creator with His design most grand,
He gave His life, the Sacrificial Lamb.
He is The Son of Man with the master plan;
Some things we're not meant to understand.

Only The LORD possesses such magnitude of mind,
For all things to come are written till the end of time;
When we are meant to be way ahead or far behind,
How long we are to live and when we enter a box of pine.

He determines the people we are and are not to meet,
Life's moments of sorrow and victories so sweet.
When He collects His church, they are promised a seat,
While the rest of the world will be destroyed by heat.

Despite having free will, GOD is the one that is in control.
The Father keeps us dry and warm or puts us out in the cold.
He decides who dies young and who gets to grow old.
He determines who enters the gate to His heavenly stronghold.

He leads us into the places that we are meant to be.
The LORD shows us the things He wants us to see.
The Holy Spirit inspires the ones He wants to lead,
But it is still our decision whether or not we believe.

We are created from earth, and our flesh returns to the dust.
Written is the smiting of the wicked and rewarding of the just.
His plans are custom-built for each and every one of us.
Only in The LORD do I place my faith and my trust.

It is written who goes unnoticed and who acquires fame,
Those of good mind and who has a problem in their brain.
He knew what would happen to Abel at the hand of Cain.
The LORD knows when we will lose and when we will gain.

Some things we are meant to know, some never to find out.
He knows the ones that will have faith and those that will doubt.
He knew that Moses would climb to the top of the mount.
It's known when our path is straight and when we need to reroute.

Sometimes we have a choice, some things are fate,
Like the one we are to marry and who we want to date.
The LORD works on His own time and can never be late,
Who gets cast down and who enters the pearly gates.

We are all His children; The Father loves us all.
His hand lifts up the poor and causes kings to fall.
When the rapture comes, His angels will stand tall,
But until then, we are waiting for the trumpet's call.

The Path to Salvation

To humbly serve The LORD is not easy to do.
The path to salvation is a daily challenge,
But if you follow the word He will guide you through,
He will never give a task that you can't manage.

To be granted salvation is its own reward,
Granted to those who praise His name.
The price to pay is one that everyone can afford.
His awesomeness is eternal and never wanes.

Every day we must praise the King of Kings.
Only in Jesus's glory we will find salvation,
His archangels spreading their heavenly wings.
Even during a famine, He saves us from starvation.

When we worship and praise the LORD,
His mercies are bestowed with abundance.
He shields us against the demonic horde,
And His blessings are given in redundance.

From the modern big cities to the tiny fishing villages,
His will be done throughout each and every land.
To achieve salvation is the highest of privileges,
Collecting His church with His outstretched hand.

The road of righteousness is a rocky road indeed.
This path is very cumbersome to walk and travel,
Spreading His word and planting His seed,
But without His glory, our world would quickly unravel.

If it were not for the blood of The Sacrificial Lamb,
We would live our lives in condemnation;
The perfect sacrifice, the magnificent Son of Man,
Saving us from our sins and eternal damnation.

To destroy the wicked, He caused the great flood.
By His mercy, He charged Noah to build the ark.
For our salvation, He spilled His blood
So we must live by His word and never part.

Anyone can believe when presented with facts,
But to live to serve The LORD requires great faith.
The adversary tries to lure us with glamorous acts.
I will earn my place in His kingdom no matter what it takes.

The Universal Solution

No matter what problems a person has in their life,
Worshiping The LORD is the universal solution.
He heals the sick, returns to the blind their sight.
Only faith and prayer can remove spiritual pollution.

Irrespective of what troubles someone has,
There is only one way to cure what ails you.
The LORD will make any and every affliction pass,
If you simply do the things He wants you to.

When His servant has a problem, He gets involved.
He causes our enemies to scatter and displace.
No quarrel or conflict The King of Kings can't resolve.
Anything that His follower has lost, The LORD will replace.

I will praise Him till my flesh falls from my bones.
His armor protects me from the demonic horde.
It's a privilege, a pleasure, and an honor all its own.
There is no enemy that can withstand His sword.

When the scripture one does read,
He turns utter chaos into tranquil stillness.
He knows and provides us with all that we need.
He can heal our wounds and takes away our illness.

There is nothing beyond His awesome power.
Songs of His glory and victory we sing.
He leads us to triumph in our darkest hour,
For salvation is what He will bring.

Sickness, hunger, and war don't stand a chance.
His blessings are as countless as the sand,
Celebrating His mercies with song and dance
Because no turmoil can prevail against His hand.

To every problem we face, He is the ultimate answer.
The LORD is loving mercy but also consuming fire.
He removes our afflictions such as cancer.
He brings joy to our heart in times most dire.

He pours His manna into our empty pot.
He nurtures us like prized crops on a farm.
We are all The LORD's children, His love we've got.
He protects us and shelters us from harm.

He takes the treasures away from the greedy.
The most wise and majestic of all nobility,
Causing one fish to feed the hungry and needy;
There is nothing outside of His capability.

To Serve and Praise

Jesus Christ is great, and He is good.
I praise Him daily like everybody should.
Every single morning, when I awake,
With hands clasped together, a knee I take.

To The LORD, my sins I humbly repent and confess,
Giving thanks and asking Him for forgiveness.
Every day, to Him, I declare my dedication.
His holy word is my spiritual medication.

I shall worship The LORD for all of my days.
He is glorious and worthy of all of my praise.
Jesus brings with Him the glory of salvation.
He is the savior of each and every nation.

For me, The Son of GOD has paid the ultimate price,
But He knew His destiny, the perfect sacrifice.
He shed His blood and gave His life for me
So that the kingdom of heaven I could see.

To praise and worship Him is the least I can do.
In the difficult times, He always pulls me through.
Doing GOD's will brings my life tremendous joy,
Like Christmas, unwrapping each day like a new toy.

There was a time when I took pleasure in sinning,
Yet I couldn't figure out why I was never winning.
Now that I know Him, my spirit is always raising,
Living with Christ in my heart I'm constantly praising.

Life is not perfect without difficulty and challenge,
But through my faith in Christ, I always manage.
Despite being raised up in a house of Jews,
It is The Father, The Son, and The Spirit I choose.

Determined not to make my parents' mistakes,
Not the path of the world but of salvation I take.
Living to serve Jesus Christ is a glorious feeling.
The blessings He gives are too great for concealing.

To live to serve The LORD is my greatest desire.
He is loving mercy, but He is also consuming fire.
Against my enemies, The LORD is my protection.
The Spirit guards me from the accuser's deception.

With love for The LORD Jesus, I have been injected.
For all my days, in my heart, He will never be rejected.
To The Savior, my life, my heart, and my soul I have dedicated;
Yet all good works in His name are tenfold reciprocated.

To worshiping His glory, I dedicate my energy and time.
One way that I praise Him is to write this poetic rhyme.
Trusting in The Father's judgment day in and day out,
I live my daily life walking by faith instead of doubt.
If you don't trust in The LORD, you need to reroute
Because serving Christ is what living life is all about.

Unexpected Gifts

When someone lives a life of faith,
The LORD will always keep them safe.
He shields us against unseen enemies.
He awards us with unexpected victories.

GOD told us, "Ask and thou shall receive,"
But in our hearts, we must truly believe.
But sometimes He blesses us with a pleasant surprise,
Unexpected gifts that are impossible to surmise.

Breakthroughs that we could never expect,
They are a reward for showing Him due respect.
Things we didn't think possible, He gives and delivers.
To those that obey His word, He is the ultimate giver.

Showing His infinite mercy instead of consuming fire,
Dispensing the deepest of all our hearts' desires,
His blessings are far too many to count,
Like an overflowing spiritual bank account.

The LORD provides the things for which we yearn,
But these rewards are not free; they must be earned.
The price of His glory is a matter of faith.
Just fill your heart with love instead of hate.

He knows our desires of which we're not even aware.
He saves us from our personal living nightmares.
The LORD is all-powerful and all-knowing.
Every day my faith and love for Him is growing.

There is nothing that is beyond GOD's power.
In His presence, our enemies are made to cower.
There is nothing that can withstand His might.
It feels amazing when you find favor in His sight.

His love is the light that shows us the right path.
Christ delivers us from out of the devil's grasp,
Bringing victory when all hope seems lost.
His will be done because He is the boss.

Always bestowing little gift I can't anticipate,
But I know a place in His kingdom will be my fate.
Sometimes we receive a blessing in disguise.
I welcome them all if it is seen as good in His eyes.

His glory is worth more than all the money in the world.
I eagerly wait to watch the grand design unfurl.
I accept whatever The LORD has in store for me.
Now that I found salvation, I'm happy as can be.

Chapter Three

SPECIAL POEMS

Books

As we know, the Bible is comprised of sixty-six books, from Genesis to Revelation. The next three poems are poetic summaries retelling the portion of the story indicated by the title. While these poems are written according to the scriptures, it is important to understand that these poems do take creative license and are, **in no way**, to be considered scripture themselves and are **not** (according to 2 Timothy 3:16) "given by inspiration of GOD, and is profitable for doctrine, for reproof, for correction, for instruction in righteousness" by any means! Their purpose is simply to be enjoyed by the reader!

Genesis 1-8

In the beginning, nothing existed until The LORD gave birth
To His first creations, which are the heavens and the earth,
But the earth was a void, formless, and totally dark.
For all that was over the water was the divine spark.
Then GOD said, "Let there be light," and He saw that it was good.
He made and divided the day and the night as only He could.

He created the firmament on the second day, and He called it heaven.
It divided the waters, and He did it in chapter one, verse number seven.
Then He created the dry land, which is earth, and called the waters seas.
He also brought forth grass herbs that yield seeds and fruit trees.

The fourth day He created in heaven the sun, moon, and the stars.
They divided night and day also so days and seasons can be marked.
On the fifth day, He filled the sea and sky with living creatures.
He said, "Be fruitful and multiply," those with wings and scaly features.

The sixth day He created the beasts of the earth and things that crawl.
Then He made man in His image and gave us dominion over them all.
He has given us every herb that yields seed and every tree its fruit.
Also every green herb He has given us all for sources of food.

But on the seventh day, GOD finished His work and decided to rest.
He then sanctified that seventh day, and by Him, it has been blessed.
GOD had put the man in the garden He planted in the land of Eden.
With pleasant-looking and edible plants, this garden was teeming,
Also the four rivers and the trees of knowledge and of life.
Adam was told he could eat from any plant but those, lest he surely die.

Adam names every bird of the air and every beast of the ground,
But among them all, a helper comparable to him was never found.
So The LORD took a rib from Adam after he was put in a deep sleep.
From that rib, He created a woman whose name would be called Eve.
This is why a man is said to be as one flesh with his wife
From the day they get married and for the rest of their life.

But one day the serpent came to them with intent to deceive.
He tricked the woman into eating the fruit from the forbidden tree.
The woman, in turn, gave the notorious fruit to her husband to eat.
Eating the fruit of knowledge, their eyes opened, and they could see.

Now they realized they were naked and took leaves to cover themselves.
When they heard GOD walking in the garden into hiding they propelled.
The LORD called out to Adam, "Where are you? Where did you go?"
Adam said he hid for he was naked, and GOD asked, "Who told you this was so?"

So He cursed the serpent to forever eat dust and crawl on his belly,
And to the woman, He made the birthing pains exceptionally heavy.
GOD cursed them that by the sweat of their brow, they may eat bread.
Now to the dust they were created from shall they return when they're dead.

Adam knew Eve and first conceived Cain, then they conceived Abel.
Cain tilled the field, while Abel kept sheep to put meat on the table.
To The LORD they brought offerings, Cain of his harvest and Abel of his flock.

The LORD was pleased with Abel but not with Cain, much to his shock.

At this, Cain grew hot with anger, and because of this, his countenance fell,
But GOD said to him, Why are you angry? Will you not be accepted if you do well?
But if you continue to do the wrong things, you will be opening the door to sin,
And it waits for you like a lion waiting to devour you, but you must not let it win.

However, the anger overcame Cain, and with rage over Abel, his heart did flood.
Cain took his brother into the midst of a field, and there he spilled Abel's blood.
As punishment, Cain was cursed to wander without a home the rest of his days,
But to protect him, GOD said, "Anyone that kills Cain shall suffer seven times as great."

Adam was the first generation, and after him had come nine more.
This ninth generation is the one to which the famous Noah had been born.
Sons of Adam, the son of GOD, had taken wives and produced a time were only evil was enjoyed.
Regretting ever creating them, all of man The LORD was going to destroy.

But Noah, Shem, Ham, Japheth, and their wives had found favor in The LORD's eyes.
Because he walked with GOD in all His ways, GOD told Noah the end was nigh.
GOD warned him of the flood and instructed him to build a massive ark.
He made sure it was big enough so with two of every animal, they can all embark.

Forty days and forty nights, the rain fell and completely flooded all the earth.

Except the one inside the ark, every living creature died that was ever given birth.

After a hundred and fifty days, the ark ceased to float, so Noah sent out a bird.

It didn't come back, and in the voice of The LORD, "Time to leave the ark," he heard.

Noah built an altar and made sacrifices of every clean bird and beast.

When GOD smelled the sweet savor, such an aromatic, fragrant feast,

The LORD vowed never to curse the ground because of man again.

Seasons shall never cease cold and heat as long as the earth remains.

Exodus 1-14

The sons of Isaac, the sons of Abraham,
To His chosen people, The LORD gave the holy land.
To the sons of Jacob, who the same is Israel,
He demonstrated GOD's might and mercy so surreal.

Moses was placed in an ark and left by the Nile.
Pharaoh's daughter laid eyes and started to smile.
Born to a Hebrew but raised with the Egyptians,
He delivered his people out of affliction.

The LORD called to him from a bush set aflame.
From that day forth, that shepherd was never the same.
Jehovah chose him to lead them to the land of Canaan.
Out from the hands of their oppressors, they will be gone.

Moses approached and requested that his people be let go,
But the arrogant pharaoh simply said no.
With his mission from GOD having been made clear
He pleaded for his people, but he was not given an ear.

From rivers of blood to frogs, lice, and flies;
A storm of hail and fire in which everything died;
Boils, locusts, darkness, and diseased cattle;
For His people, with wondrous acts, He did battle.

Against all these plagues, Pharaoh's heart was hardened,
But to the final one, he was forced to hearken.
The LORD passed through the land by night.
Every firstborn Egyptian son, The LORD did smite.

With the death of his son, even the king of Egypt had no choice.
He was forced to listen to the message of Aaron's voice.
He let them go as per his decree, but he just could not let them be.
The Egyptian chariots pursued till they were pressed to the sea.

Led by a pillar of cloud during the day and a pillar of fire by night,
Jehovah directed the children of Israel by His miraculous signs.
As per Jehovah's command, Moses stretched out the rod in his hand.
He made the waters disband and gave means to cross on dry land.

On their king's orders, the Egyptian army did chase and pursue
But delivered was the seed of Abraham, which is the Hebrews.
The waters rose up as a wall on the left and on the right,
Then crashed down on their oppressors, not one left alive.

Matthew 1-3

1

The genealogy of Jesus, called the Son of Man,
Also called the Son of David, Son of Abraham,
From Abraham to David and David to Babylon, then to the birth of
our King;
Each one of these space, a measure of generations fourteen.
Mary, while a virgin, was with a child by the Holy Spirit.
Joseph, her husband, was thinking what to do about it,
But an angel of The LORD came to him in a dream.
Do not be afraid, for by The Holy Spirit, she has conceived.
She will bear a son whom you shall call Jesus,
Also known as Immanuel, meaning God with us.

2

When He was born, there came kings from the east,
Searching for the One holier than the priests.
When King Herod heard this, in his heart, he mourned.
He inquired all the priests and scribes where this child was born.
Herod asked the wise men to bring him word when the child was found.
They set out and following the star above Him who was on the ground.
They arrived at the manger, bringing frankincense, myrrh, and gold.
They were divinely warned about Herod, so they took a new route home.
Joseph departed with Jesus and Mary, and to Egypt, they left.
When Herod found out, he had all male babies put to their death.
As per the angel's instructions, in Egypt, they did patiently wait,

Until the angel of The LORD appeared and told Joseph it was safe,
But on their way to Israel, they were warned that Herod's son was king,
So they diverted to Galilee so that it may be fulfilled. "He shall be
called a Nazarene."

3

In those days, John the Baptist roamed the wilderness in Judea land,
Everywhere declaring, "Repent, for the kingdom of heaven is at hand!"
Wearing raiment of camel's hair, eating locusts and wild honey,
John prepared the way of The LORD; he didn't think it was funny,
Baptizing people in the Jordan, from throughout the region.
But when the Pharisees came, he cried "generation of vipers" for good
reason.
John told the people, "Now also the ax laid unto the root."
Into the fire will be cast "every tree which bringeth not forth good
fruit."
"I baptize with water, but I say that One comes after me that is higher."
"It is He that will baptize you with The Holy Ghost and with fire."
Then Jesus came and was baptized, and the heavens opened above.
A great light shone, and the Holy Spirit descended upon Him like a
dove.
"This is my beloved Son, in whom I am well pleased," The Father said
in love.

Christmas

As the title of this section of Chapter 3 suggests, the following three poems are Christmas poems. However, what may or not be evident is that these were poems I wrote as part of a custom-created Christmas card to be given out at my church and to whomever else.

Christmas 2016

Even though to the faith I might still be sort of new, that won't stop me from wishing a Merry Christmas to you.

I wish you all the joy The Holy Spirit brings this season. Why we can rejoice today and forever, Jesus is the reason.

This celebrated day that The Word became flesh.

He descended to the earth, a child holier than all the rest.

For this was the time The Father poured out His divine favor.

He gave us His only begotten Son, Jesus Christ our Savior.

Let us come together to rejoice in the coming of The LORD.

For only Jesus is worthy to be worshiped and adored.

As we remember this wonderful Christmas story,

Let us fellowship and give unto GOD all the glory.

May His praises continually be upon all our lips.

May His written word never be far from our fingertips.

So at this time, and with this rhyme, what I want to say

Is that I pray that you have a blessed Christmas Day.

May peace, grace, and love of The LORD surround you and your loved ones this Christmas 2016.

GOD BLESS YOU!

Christmas 2017

Christmas is the time we commemorate the glorious day
That our Savior Jesus Christ came to earth as a baby to reign.
The LORD always knows how to give the most perfect of gifts,
Glorious signs and wonders that when in need, our spirits He lifts.

GOD so loved the world that He gave His only begotten Son
So that the power of sin over man can be forever undone.
Jesus is the Father's gift that keeps on giving since His birth;
All the gold, silver, and precious gems cannot equal His worth.

He gives us mercy, grace, peace, joy, authority, wisdom, and freedom.
He gave us His life and prepares a mansion for us in His kingdom.
He performs miracles and healings to those of every tongue and nation.
He provides abundantly and gives the greatest of all gifts—salvation.

GOD loves us so much He wants to keep us eternally living.
That is why He gave us Jesus, the gift that keeps on giving.
So I pray that you have a merry and blessed Christmas Day.
May The LORD grant you all a Christmas blessing in Jesus's name.

Christmas 2018

Praying for you a blessed Christmas of twenty eighteen.
May this begin a new season, miraculous and divinely serene.
I pray for an abundance of blessings like you've never seen.
May living waters flow from your belly in an unending stream.

I pray a new chapter of blessing in your life for Him to start,
That the peace of GOD always keep your mind and heart.
May an outpouring of The Holy Spirit power upon you He impart,
That from your presence, the wicked one shall fearfully depart.

May the Prince of Peace heal every pain and dry every tear.
May the perfect love of The LORD cast out all doubt and fear.
I pray that our Savior will bless you in a mighty way this year.
May Jesus give you a new testimony for everyone to hear.

Let Him place upon you a brand new robe and a brand new ring.
Let Him hide you under the shadow of His majestic wing.
Let Him bring you blessings that only Jesus Christ can bring.
I declare all these blessings in the name of Jesus, our King.

In Loving Memory

This is the shortest chapter, only having two poems. However, as the chapter title indicates, these poems were written "in loving memory" of two people whom The LORD called home to glory after my salvation. These poems attempt to express how much they are missed and will continue to be greatly missed until the day The LORD calls me home also.

One More Chance

In loving memory of Bro. Jesus Cruz,
Risen to glory on May 15, 2018.

If only we knew your appointed date and time,
We could have said our best and final goodbye;
O for one more chance your smiling face to see,
O for one more chance for another memory.

If only we could share with you one more joke,
O how we would laugh, the fun we'd poke.
If only one more chance to give you a big hug
And express to you the magnitude of our love.

If only one more chance, a story we could share.
If only one more chance to say how much we care;
If only one more chance for even just one more day
To say all the things we now wish we could say.

If only one more chance to say how we felt;
If only one more chance to say farewell;
If only one more chance to say how much you'll be missed
Before you are forever with Christ in glory and heavenly bliss.

But now you're rewarded for all the good you've sown,
For now The LORD has seen fit to call you home.
Rejoice **I**n **P**aradise, ye good and faithful servant.
Rejoice **I**n **P**aradise, by GOD's grace you deserve it!

Mournful Rejoice

In loving memory of my mother Lynn Solomon,
Risen to glory on August 8, 2018.

I, with a heavy heart, saturated with mournful rejoice,
Remember my beloved mother in glory with The Son.
The LORD called her home, we were not given a choice,
But we trust our Father; let His will, not ours, be done.

Many memories together will I always commemorate.
My earthly loss has become her glorious heavenly gain.
This is why with mournful rejoice for her, I celebrate
Because she is now free from all affliction, tears, and pain.

With each memory, a bitter sweet sorrow fills my heart.
A cocktail of wrenching pain and joy fall from our eyes,
For she was called home and out of my sight did depart,
Mournfully rejoicing that my mother ascended to the skies.

We all will leave friends and family behind here on earth below.
No matter how much it hurts, we can't keep those we love.
Taking comfort in mournful rejoice, there's one thing we know:
We are thankful for salvation, we will dwell with Christ above.

With mournful rejoice, I miss my mother incredibly.
With mournful rejoice, I cherish every single memory.
I mournfully rejoice, and I know it is only temporarily,
For my mournfulness ends when I rejoice with her in the heavenly.

Occasions

This chapter contains poems which were written for various occasions. Three of them were written for the holidays of Thanksgiving, Mother's Day, and Father's Day, respectively, as will be evident by their titles. One, which is also evident by title, was written for my baptism service, and the last poem in this section was penned as a poetic farewell to a congregation I left to begin attending my current church.

G.I.V.E.T.H.A.N.K.S.

G-ratitude is the right attitude,
 for humility is the key to spiritual altitude.

I-n all things, give thanks and supplication;
 be a joyful demonstration of holy communication.

V-ictory in Jesus we gain only through Calvary's pain;
 that eternal life in heaven, we can attain.

E-ver present, His presence is so pleasant;
 tomorrow not promised each day His present.

T-o The LORD, we must be grateful, for He is able;
 He never forsakes us, for He is faithful.

H-allelujah, Jesus! You will never leave us.
 Of our fears pains and sickness, You relieve us.

A-lmighty GOD, Who is, Who was, and is yet to come,
 He is The Holy One who victory over hell has won.

N-ever tired of His presence, it is hence
 I express my thanks in present, past, and future tense.

K-ind and blessed Savior, His love can never waver;
 by changes of heart, He removes ungodly behavior.

S-avior, The Truth, The Way, and The Life, You are our marvelous light.
 We give all the glory and G.I.V.E.T.H.A.N.K.S. to Christ tonight.

Moms And Mothers

Mothers are the women through whom into the world we came,
In whose womb we were fearfully and wonderfully made.
Little babies in her arms, we continue to develop and grow;
Feeding us, changing us, and bathing us from head to tiny toe.

Dressing us in cute little outfits we don't appreciate at the time,
Making sure we are warm enough and covering our behind,
Laying us down in our cribs and tucking us in tight,
Enjoying the few hours their baby actually sleeps at night.

They teach us to walk and get dressed on our own.
They teach us to talk and use the bathroom all alone.
As we get older and learn to do things for ourselves,
There is even more things with which we rely on their help.

Making sure we get up in time and are not late for school,
Teaching us to be obedient and follow the rules,
Making sure our homework gets done at night,
Getting us in bed no matter how hard we fight.

Mothers do their best to provide for their kids.
A mother protects her child as long as she lives,
And one day that child will learn to appreciate.
Maybe one day they will actually reciprocate.

Mothers are great, but moms aren't quite the same.
Mothers attend to our needs, but moms sit and play games.
Mothers teach us to behave and give discipline.
Moms take us to the park, having fun and whistling.

Moms are our first friends, and to our feeling, they tend.
For us, backwards they bend and are there until the end.
Moms also tickle us till we wheeze and playfully tease
But cover scraped knees to keep them clean from disease.

Moms are there when we need someone to talk to.
Even when she's mad, a mom will always love you.
Though she may not like certain choices you make,
A mom accepts you as you are; her love is not at stake.

A mom is the first woman that will come in your life.
She will influence how you choose your future wife.
She likes laughing, telling jokes, and kidding around.
A mom is a woman who turns your frown upside down.

A mom will teach you tricks from when she was young,
Imparting her wisdom to her daughter and sons.
Even in those moments when we are angry and want to run,
Our love for our moms and mothers shall never come undone.
Let us honor our moms and mothers until His Kingdom come.

My Baptism Poem

Today I dedicate my heart and soul to Jesus Christ
because for my salvation, He gave His life.
From youth, into spiritual darkness I was hurled,
but in 2014, Jesus entered and illuminated my world.
Since then I've never been the same,
a new creation forevermore changed.
Today I come to renounce and bury the old me
so The Holy Spirit I may receive.
I confess GOD resurrected Jesus in holy accord
and declare to the world that Jesus is LORD.

My Fathers

A father is a man who is there to share his wisdom and knowledge.
A father is willing to sacrifice things; they want to send you to college.
Giving guidance and doing their part to send you on the right path,
They are people that make sure what you need, you will have.

In my life, there are a few people that have stepped into this role,
People that have kept me cool when I was about to lose control,
People to provide answers when I am not sure how to proceed.
A father is like a teacher whose words should always be well received.

I have been blessed with a few father figures that correct mistakes.
Though not related by blood, this role they decided to undertake.
To assume this leadership role is a job that is not always easy,
Especially my real father who brings me an inhaler when I'm wheezy.

For me, family has nothing to do with blood or genetics.
It's the people whose love has an energy most kinetic.
Family are those that are there for you in time of need.
A father is someone whose wise counsel you should gladly receive.

The first such person that came in to my life is my brother,
My best friend and far wiser, but born to another mother.
The most recent of these respectable men is now my pastor,
Greatly respected who I'm certain will save me from disaster.

But I haven't yet mentioned the most important and significant Father.
With all the wisdom of the others combined, He far smarter.
He is the path, the fact, and the spark; the ender and the starter;
The One who gave His only begotten Son to be our living martyr

He is The Heavenly Father to each and every living soul that has breath.
He is The One that, in times of war and turmoil, can provide us with
rest,
The Father that created everything on earth that has ever existed.
Even though His will, many of His creations are continually resisting.

If you haven't figured it out by now, this Father is The Mighty Jehovah,
Our LORD and GOD whose loving kindness and mercy runneth over.
He has blessed me with father figures but none compare to El Shaddai.
Not any man or accumulation, thereof, that can equal our GOD Most
High.

My earthly fathers, I will respect until the very last of all my days.
But none of them are worthy to be worshiped and exalted with praise.
For these people are very important to me beyond a shadow of a doubt.
But it is only my Father sitting on heaven's throne that I can't live
without.

I spend the day with my Heavenly Father with praise. In His house, I
am a winner.
Then in the evening, I will see my earthly father and later maybe go
out for dinner.
But I will never forget *all* of these men who have made such a difference,
The father figures that have taught me how to overcome life's hindrance.
So this Father's Day, I celebrate all of my fathers, Him in heaven and
those on earth,
Especially the two that without *them*, my mother would have never
given birth.

The LORD Is Calling

The LORD has taken me from a place of evil, darkness, and violence.
He has removed me from a state of engaging in joyful malevolence.
He has removed from me a joy of pouring out my wrath,
And He called me to walk upon the straight and narrow path.

The LORD called me out of a life of spiritual and physical crime.
In Him, I'm a new creation, praising Him all the time.
He chose me to relate to people, all tattooed, drunken, and hostile;
But because I was like them, I'm able to bring them the gospel.

The easy path is wide, and it has many twists and turns.
It revisits places of pleasure and to familiarity usually returns,
But walking the straight and narrow is doing what is difficult.
It has pit stops of comfort, but to growth in faith and wisdom, it catapults.

Verily, Christ has called me to drop my net and follow Him,
To take with me only memories from places where I've been.
To follow my destiny, I needed to leave many things behind.
This includes people, places, old habits and states of mind.

To become the person The LORD created to fulfill my destiny,
I must at times give up those with who I want to be,
Forfeiting pleasures, comforts, and habits that breed vice,
For my eternal reward, for my Salvation, I am willing to sacrifice.

GOD brings me to many places each having their purpose,
Sometimes it's obvious, and others the reason lay under the surface.
He leads us on our path, where to go He does mention.
But His will be done, it's not our place to question.

He calls us to leave places that we would like to stay,
But when and to where He calls us, we must obey.
Although I'd rather stay where I am having fun,
The LORD has told me that my work *here* is now done.

The LORD has sent me for the many lessons I have learned
To see and to hear and to observe; He has sent me to sojourn,
And now the time has come, the future is calling me
To take these lessons and continue along with my destiny.

For not even the apostles and disciples stood in one place
But traveled from place to place preaching amazing grace.
Some people are called to plant their feet and stabilize,
But Christ has called me to go all over to evangelize.

Though I'd like to plant my feet, I must be uprooted,
For there is none other than Jesus Christ to be saluted.
I have enjoyed my experience here with all of you,
But The LORD is calling me, so I must bid you adieu.

Prayer Poems

This chapter is perhaps the most unique chapter of the book, as all four of the poems are prayers, which I have actually used and prayed over myself and for others. I would encourage the reader to also utilize these prayers to pray over people or circumstances that they might apply to. Furthermore, two of the four are written in Spanish. For those who are not able to understand Spanish, I have also followed the original version with an English translation. Obviously, the English version will not have the same poetic attributes or rhythmic flow as the original; however, it will give the reader a grasp of the prayer and enable them to still use these prayers.

A New Chapter

We praise Thee for Thou art GOD, and there is none like Thee,
Declaring from the beginning things that are not yet done.
You are The Father, The Word, and Spirit the Holy Trinity.
Witnessed on earth, The Spirit and the water, three agree in One.

We give thanks to Thee, O LORD, and call upon Thy name.
We make known Thine deeds among the people.
Send forth Thy consuming Holy Spirit flame
And cleanse Thou our heart, soul, and mind of all evil.

O GOD of glory, descend from the heavens above.
Thy salvation delivers us from the soul stealer.
Saturate this place with Thy blood and agape love.
O glorious GOD, Thou alone art our Healer.

Come, great LORD of all creation, and move by Thy Spirit.
Breathe the breath of life granting a new chapter to this story.
Let the fullness of Thy power manifest that nothing inhibit.
We exalt the name of Jesus that Thou receive all the glory.

Touching this thing we stand in agreement on earth,
In every heart here, let the truth of Thy kingdom reign.
Unto salvation, bring death to sin that there be spiritual rebirth.
We ask this, Father, with thanksgiving in Jesus's name.

Declaro guerra (en El Nombre de Jesús)

1. Dar Gloria al Padre, El Hijo y El Espíritu Santo.
Todo el tiempo a Dios, canciones que canto.
Alabo al Señor con todo el corazón y el alma.
Su presencia me conforta y me hace la calma.

2. Luchando por el bien, de servicio dedicado a mi rey.
Porque Dios es bueno todo el tiempo, esto lo sé.
Soy un soldado de la salvación, un hijo del Dios Altísimo.
Hago la Guerra en El Nombre de El Rey de Reyes, Jesus Cristo.

3. Fuego del Espíritu Santo descienda a mi y estar conmigo.
Recompensar mi fe mientras camino contigo.
Cubrirme y Proteger A Mí Como un abrigo.
Espíritu Santo protegerme de mi enemigo.

4. Los hijos de la luz vigilantes para preparar.
Y las fuerzas del mal nunca pueden ganar.
Con Nuestro Señor y Salvador ya ha ganado.
El diablo y todos sus servidores Él está destruyendo.

5. En contra de el diablo yo declaró El sangre de Jesucristo.
De mis enemigos, preparate porque no estbas listo.
Permitar que el diablo para ganar, no puedo hacerlo.
Los trabajadores de la iniquidad de DISPERSIÓN POR EL FUEGO!

6. Contra potestades y principados Declaró LA GUERRA!
El día del juicio del diablo MORIR y vamos a la fiesta.
Yo apago los dardos de fuego con el escudo de la fe.
Cuando el diablo vio la derrota, de vuelta al infierno se fue.

7. Demonios y diablos te ordeno AHORA PARA SALIR!
En el infierno que todos malos están condenados a dormir.
Contra todo lo que se oponen los niños de El Señor.
Te mando un santo DESTRUCCIÓN de los mejores.

8. Todos los hijos de Belial NO intentan TRATAR!
Pero para su DESTRUCCIÓN estar listo para PREPARAR!
VOLVERÁ sobre sus cabezas sus esfuerzos para matar!
POR EL PODER EN EL NOMBRE DE JESUCRISTO ME
MANDAN A QUEMAR!
En Jesús PODEROSO nombre rezo. Amén.

ENGLISH TRANSLATION

I Declare War (In the Name of Jesus)

1. Give glory to the Father, Son, and Holy Spirit.
All the time, to GOD, I am singing songs.
I praise The LORD with all my heart and soul.
His presence comforts me and makes me calm.

2. Fighting for good, in dedicated service to my King,
Because GOD is good all the time, that I know.
I am a soldier of salvation, a child of The Most High GOD.
I wage war in the name of The King of Kings, Jesus Christ.

3. Holy Spirit fire descend upon me and be with me.
Reward my faith as I walk with you.
Cover me and protect me as a coat.
Holy Spirit, protect me from my enemy.

4. The children of the light are vigilant to prepare.
The forces of evil can never win.
For our LORD and Savior has already won.
The devil and all his servants, He is destroying.

5. Against the devil, I claim the blood of Jesus Christ.
To my enemies, prepare yourselves, for you are not ready.
To permit the devil to win, I cannot.
Workers of iniquity *scatter by fire*!

6. Against powers and principalities, I declare *war*!
In the day of judgment, the devil will *die,* and we will celebrate.
I extinguish the flaming arrows with the shield of faith.
When the devil saw his defeat, back to hell he went.

7. Devils and demons, I command you *now to leave.*
In hell, all evil ones are condemned to sleep.
Against all devils and demons that oppose the children of the LORD,
I command a holy *destruction* of the highest (kind).

8. All ye children of Belial, do *not* attempt *to try*!
But for *destruction* to be ready to *prepare*!
Return upon their heads their efforts to kill!
By the power in the name of Jesus Christ, I *command you to burn!*
In Jesus's *mighty* name, I pray. Amen.

Mi Librador

Te damos gloria y honra de Su Padre, por todo nuestras días.
En Tus manos poderosos estamos poniendo nuestras vidas.
Hágase Tu voluntad como en el cielo, así en la tierra.
Todo el mundo es Tuyo desde los mares a la sierra.

Me has salvado de la oscuridad de este mundo.
Tú eres el primero y todo lo demás es segundo.
Te alabo Padre por todas las cosas que has hecho por mí.
Te agradezco Padre bendito por traerme cerca de Ti.

Jesucristo, Tu eres El Cordero del DIOS y El León de Judá.
"Oh Dios, no Te apartes de mí, Dios mío, apúrate mi ayuda." (Psa
71:12)
Líbrame de todas las aflicciones del enemigo.
Jehová me ayude a caminar en justicia contigo.

Los salmos dice "El nombre del SEÑOR es una torre fuerte.
El justo corre hacia ella, y está seguro." (Pro 18:10)
Quita de nosotros cuyos salarios son la muerte.
Nos entregamos nuestros corazones a Ti y nuestro futuro.

"Si Dios es por nosotros, quién puede estar en contra de nosotros?"
(Rom 8:31)
Protégeme de la gente en mi vida que tiene corazones malvados.
Refugíame de todo la gente que robará mi paz.
Deja que las tormentas de la vida roban mi alegría no más.

"Líbrame de la opresión del hombre; así guardaré Tus preceptos." (Psa 119:134)

Oh Jehová rinda los planes de los que están contra mí ineptos.

"Considera mi aflicción, y líbrame, porque no me olvido de Tu ley." (Psa 119:153)

Extiende Tu poderoso brazo y defiende mi DIOS y mi Rey.

Como has librado a Israel de los egipcios que buscaban su destrucción.

Levántate, oh SEÑOR de los ejércitos, y sálvame de mi persecución.

"Asiste a mi clamor; Líbrame de mis perseguidores; Porque son más fuertes que yo."(Psa 142:6)

Cúbreme y rodéame en la gloria protectora de Tu Espíritu Santo fuego.

Oh Elohim, "Ninguna arma que se forme contra ti prosperará" es la verdad de Tu palabra. (Isa 54:17)

Por eso Te adoramos y Te reverenciamos y Te damos la toda la gloria y el honor y toda la alaba.

Yo reclamo la sangre del Cordero contra todos los que tratan dividir a mi familia.

En el nombre de Jesucristo pisé sobre estas cabezas serpientes, conquista y concilia.

En el nombre glorioso y victorioso de Jesucristo de Nazaret, El Rey Resucitado rezo. Amén.

My Deliverer

We give glory and honor to You, Father, for all our days.
In Your powerful hands, we are putting our lives.
Thy will be done as in heaven, so on earth.
Everything is Yours, from the seas to the mountain ranges.

You have saved me from the darkness of this world.
You are first, and everything else is second.
I praise You, Father, for all the things You have done for me.
I thank You, Blessed Father, for bringing me near to You.

Jesus Christ, You are The Lamb of GOD and The Lion of Judah.
"O God, do not depart from me, my GOD, make haste for my help"
(Psalms 71:12)
Deliver me of all the afflictions of the enemy.
Jehovah, help me to walk in righteousness with you.

O LORD, help me to walk in righteousness with You.
The psalms say, "The name of the LORD is a strong tower.
The righteous runs to it, and is saved." (Proverbs 18:10)
Rid us of those whose wages are death.
We surrender to You our hearts and our future.

"If GOD is for us, who can stand against us?" (Romans 8:31)
Protect me from the people in my life who have evil hearts.
Shelter me from all the people who will steal my peace.
Let the storms of life steal my joy no more.

"Deliver me from the oppression of man: so will I keep thy precepts."
(Psalms 119:134)

O LORD, render the plans of those whom stand against me inept.

"Consider mine affliction, and deliver me: for I do not forget Thy law."
(Psalms 119:153)

Stretch forth Your mighty arm and defend me, my GOD and my King.

As You have delivered Israel from the Egyptians who sought their destruction,

Arise, O mighty LORD of hosts, and rescue me from my persecution.

"Attend to my cry; Deliver me from my persecutors; For they are mightier than I." (Psalms 142:6)

Cover me and surround me in the protective glory of Your Holy Spirit fire.

O Elohim, "No weapon that is formed against you shall prosper" is the truth of Your word. (Isaiah 54:17)

That's why we worship and revere You, give You all the glory and honor and all the praise.

I claim the blood of The Lamb against all who aim to divide my family.

In Jesus Christ's name, I tread on these serpents' heads, conquer and conciliate.

In the glorious and victorious name of Jesus Christ of Nazareth, The Risen King, I pray. Amen.

Trust and Surrender

I will trust in You, Jesus, The Son of Man.
I place my entire life into Your loving hands.
I surrender to You my will and every desire.
For I know Your plans for me are far higher.

Your word says, "Hope deferred maketh the heart sick."
You say, "But when the desire cometh, it is a tree of life."
Give me wisdom to discern to which things to stick.
Lead me away from those things that will cause strife.

I declare this day that I have made the decision
To yield in blind faith and obedient submission.
O my LORD and my GOD, I surrender unto Thee
My own desires and my will to Your majesty.

The things I want, rely on my own understanding,
But I fully trust in Your plans for me longstanding.
My own desires are limited by human imprecision.
So I prepare my heart for Your abundant provision.

Help me, Jesus, to forfeit what my eyes perceive.
That the things You purposed for me, I can receive.
Abba Father, as Your heir, I do rightfully claim
All that You desire for me in Jesus's glorious name!

Amen.

R.O.E.

This final chapter contains three poems from my first book published in 2012 titled A Rainbow Of Emotions, hence the chapter title acronym. Although this first book was also a poetry book, ROE was scribed during a period I call my "confused era." This was a period of several years preceding my salvation in 2104, when I was attempting to, as Jesus called it, "serve two masters." Therefore, the vast majority of *ROE* does not reflect the writings of a GOD-fearing Christian.

These three selected poems, however, are from the "Blue" (righteousness) and "Green" (spirituality) chapters that show a heart that is honestly seeking The LORD.

My Spiritual Journey

I was born into a culture to which I never belonged or believed.
At an early age, I realized it was not the right path for me.
Both my mother and father, practitioners of the Judaic faith,
They only keep the traditions because that's how they were raised.

It was all that I knew, so I played along to keep face.
They still don't understand the difference between religion and race.
By the age of ten, I secretly renounced all I was told.
Knowing nothing else, Judaism I gave up and atheism I did uphold.

I believed in science and what could be proved over and over again.
That lasted for a while, but there were things that science just couldn't explain.
I knew there was something out there in which all religion had its roots.
I knew there was some divine power that lies beyond fact and tangible proof.

But knowing only what I was taught as a kid,
I simply believed in GOD, but no religion I picked.
I knew only two paths but followed none, for they were not right.
I was confused, but for the answers to my questions, I did fight.

Then as I searched for a spiritual path to call my own,
I came across something interesting, the religions of old,
Not being limited to one deity, but they had many.
How was I to choose the one for me when then I didn't have any?

Then the concept of polytheism began to make sense.
Every aspect of life was controlled by a different god or goddess.
So into the world of paganism I began to inquire.
At first, I began to pour belief into water, earth, wind, and fire.

Then as time went on and I learned more,
I found there were so many other things to explore.
Then one day, in the New Aged section in the bookstore,
I found a new faith to which my attention was lured.

It was a pagan religion of worldwide practice,
But there were only two deities, a god and a goddess.
The Wiccan motto is "Harm none do as ye will."
So to one with a kind heart, it seemed to fit the bill.

At age fifteen, I adopted the Wiccan faith.
Little did I know it would just open a gate.
This religion incorporated the practice of magick.
An art of gaining desires or protecting against the tragic.
Many things I needed to construct: my altar,
My robe, my symbols, and a bowl of water;
Candles of different colors, one of them white;
My magic wand and my ceremonial knife.

All these tools I used to focus my spiritual energy.
After doing these rituals, impressive results did I see.
After a while, I got used to having this newfound power.
I used it to help myself and my loved ones in their needy hours.

It was at the age of sixteen I met my brother.
I soon found out he was like no other.
Some unknown force compelled me to start to conversate.
I didn't know it then, but I know now it was our fate.

For some reason, I asked, "Where can I get a pentagram to wear on my chest?"
Much to surprise, he moved his book, and there was one drawn on his desk.
He practiced magic, but he was no Wiccan,
For he was a magician who was indulging in sin.

A student of the world with this curiosity of mine,
I wanted to learn more to see what it was like.
He let me listen to music and shared many simple things.
He became my teacher and took me under his wing.

It became about having fun and indulging my every desire.
As a teenage youth, it was a concept I couldn't help but admire.
I remember when I made my first attack,
Using not white, but magic black.

There was a girl who embarrassed me well.
The very next day, down the stairs she fell,
Using only a string tied with special knots.
During her fall, she broke her arms and hurt it lots.

From that day on, I cast spells of good and bad.
I make my friends happy and my enemies sad.
One day my brother and I went to the woods upstate.
Bonded by blood and spirit, we can never separate.

For the blood that flows within our veins,
In both him and I are now one and the same.
For several years, we did the devil's work.
Many victims, but never an innocent hurt.

Until one day the demons that we employed
Came within and took our bodies for their own joy.
For once, they were welcome, like a close friend,
But welcoming them nearly brought me to my end.

For torment and torture is what they do.
We both knew, with them, we had to be through.
We went to a Christian church one night.
An exorcism was performed, and the demons took flight.

That was the first time I truly felt the presence of The LORD.
That was the time I said goodbye to the demonic horde.
The power of The Holy Ghost flowed within me.
The mistakes of blasphemy were then clear for me to see.

Blanketed in the softest of white light,
Tranquil serenity, a truly blissful delight,
Such a surreal experience of love and peace,
A taste of heaven, my own little piece.

The amazing feeling that I experienced inside,

I will need a whole book of poems just to describe.
Even though I had not read the Bible through,
From that day forth, His glory I surely knew.

I threw out symbols, talismans, candles, and books.
When I was done, my room had an empty look.
With all the teachings, experience, and knowledge,
It was as if I had attended spiritual college.

But I soon realized this knowledge was meant to be.
With all these skills I've learned, now I can see
All the acts of evil, corruption, and all the blasphemies
Allow me to better understand and defeat the adversary.

Now I am a servant of The LORD, upholding my Christian faith,
Celebrating The LORD, and keeping my loved ones safe.
No longer do I commit blasphemous acts of sin
But rather use the word of GOD to protect my kin.

Serving my King even in the moments I feel jaded,
Praising His name, and giving thanks for all that He created,
This concept may be misunderstood by most.
I am a humble servant of The Father, Son, and Holy Ghost.
A soldier and servant of The LORD I have become,
Serving The King of Kings till His kingdom come.

Soldiers Sacrifice

Always fighting the good fight,
Always doing what is known to be right;
Sacrificing of yourself for those you meet,
Searching for the strength to stand on your feet.

When GOD is the only one you serve,
You know in the end, you'll get what you deserve.
Although your life may be surrounded by sin,
No matter the afflictions, you can never give in.

Putting the needs of others before your own,
Standing up for what's right even if you stand alone,
Doing for others more than myself,
It's the innocent people I'm here to help.

Altruism to others is what I know,
All my work and nothing to show,
But I don't do it for material gain.
I don't do it for fortune and fame.

Since youth, I've been blessed with a gift.
People in times of need, their spirits I lift.
I have close friends that will always be there for me,
But what I long for most is to start my own family.

To be a servant of The LORD is to not follow the crowd.
To be a soldier is to want to scream but make not a sound.
Service to others brings to the heart such great joy
But also sorrow having never a child, a girl or a boy.

Every person has hopes and dreams,
But those of my own, impossible it once seemed.
Everyone is here for a reason, of that I am sure,
But season after season, this loneliness I endure.

Always giving and giving and very little back I take.
Perhaps the pain of this earth is my key to heaven's gate.
Living a life of selflessness, honor, and praise,
For the glory of GOD, steadfast to His call I raise.

Most people never know what He has in store to be.
Their part in the grand design, they may never see,
But to His will, I will always do my best to stay true.
If living for others is why I am here, then that is what I shall do.

This earth is not heaven, though His kingdom draws near.
When my life on earth is done, it will be worth all my tears.
So until the day comes when He comes to collect his church,
Service to others shall soothe my heart from this loneliness curse.

The LORD has blessed me with good people that make me smile.
Serving The LORD is what makes my life worthwhile.
For The LORD has given to comfort my pain.
A few true friends for which I may do the same.

One day He shall bless me with someone to hold.
One day He shall bless me with a woman with a heart of gold,
But it is all part of the grand design,
And one day He will give me a sign.

For my bride to be, I must patiently wait
Until the day He sees fit to introduce my soul mate,
And even after He has finally given me a wife,
To The LORD I will always dedicate my life.

Warrior of Light

It's a crazy world we live in,
A world full of sin.
It's evil around every bend,
Seems like the good can never win.

But it's not about who has more might.
It's about fighting the good fight,
Not concerned what the world thinks,
Just doing what you know is right.

A warrior of light is never alone,
Though he may be flesh and bone.
When judgment day comes,
The warrior will be welcomed home.

Against the evils of old,
The warrior of light stands bold,
For in the heat of battle,
His warm heart grows cold.

A life of morality and pride,
The warrior doesn't hide,
And when his nature is challenged,
The warrior takes the noble side.

When life's road gets rough
And the conditions get tough,
The warrior looks deep inside
And finds faith is reason enough.

A "normal life" is not his fate.
Pain and sacrifices he must take,
But what he has given up
Will be worth entering heaven's gate.

Not first choice the life he lives,
But his mind stays positive,
For he knows his place in this world.
His help and protection he gives.

He might like the life he has,
But he plays along like the jazz.
One note after the next,
He creates the things that give it zaz.
Things he'll never have he desires,
But the need for them is not dire.
For serving, helping, and protecting,
It's what truly lights his fire.

By most he may not be accepted,
But with morality he's been infected.
Although he fights for those who can't,
His perfection was never expected.

His tale seems one of exaggeration,
But it's a tale of true dedication.
To understand his view of the world,
It requires very much contemplation.

So much of himself he truly gave.
So many people he tried to save.
His reward lies in his heart and soul,
For his hands remain unpaid.

His struggle is for the good of man.
To serve The LORD he does what he can.
Living the life of a warrior of light
Is a lifestyle most can't understand.

CPSIA information can be obtained
at www.ICGtesting.com
Printed in the USA
BVHW071151191219
567196BV00001B/126/P

9 781796 076028